Backyard Animals

Opossums

Christine Webster

Weigl Publishers Inc.

Published by Weigl Publishers Inc.
350 5th Avenue, Suite 3304, PMB 6G
New York, NY 10118-0069
Website: www.weigl.com

Library of Congress Cataloging-in-Publication Data

Webster, Christine.
  Opossums / Christine Webster.
      p. cm. -- (Backyard animals)
  Includes index.
  ISBN 978-1-59036-677-6 (hard cover : alk. paper) -- ISBN 978-1-59036-678-3 (soft
cover : alk. paper)
  1. Opossums--Juvenile literature. I. Title.

QL737.M34W43 2008
599.2'76--dc22

                                                    2006102107

Printed in the United States of America
  2 3 4 5 6 7 8 9 0 11 10 09 08

Editor Heather C. Hudak
Design and Layout Terry Paulhus

Cover: Opossums have lived on Earth for about 70 million years. They are some
of the world's oldest living mammals.

Contents

Meet the Opossum

The term "playing possum" comes from an animal called an opossum. An opossum pretends to be dead if it is cornered by a **predator**. It rolls over, shuts its eyes, and sticks out its tongue. The opossum can lie still for hours. When the predator leaves, the opossum stops playing dead.

An opossum is a type of **mammal** called a marsupial. At birth, marsupials are not well developed. For many weeks, they live and eat in a pouch on their mother's belly. Other marsupials include the koala bear and the kangaroo.

Opossums are the size of a large house cat. Most are covered with gray fur. Their pointed faces are white with a pink nose. They have hairless black ears. Opossums can be 7 to 41 inches (17 to 104 centimeters) long, including their tail.

Some South American opossums do not have pouches.

Baby opossums spend about two months inside their mother's pouch before moving about on their own.

All about Opossums

There are about 65 opossum **species**. Most species live in Central and South America. The Virginia opossum is the largest species of opossum. It is found in North America.

Opossums live in many different **habitats**. Some live in grassy areas. Others live in rain forests. Many species spend much of their time in trees. One species is aquatic. This means it spends most of its time in the water.

Australia is home to an animal called the possum. It may be a distant relative of the opossum. The brushtail possum is an example of this species.

Opossum Facts

Virginia Opossum

- The only marsupial mammal in North America
- The most common opossum

Yapok

- Also known as the water opossum
- Lives near rivers and streams in Central and South America
- Has webbed hind feet for swimming

Bushy-tailed Opossum

- Found in South America
- Tail is almost completely covered with fur

Western Woolly Opossum

- Found in Mexico, and Central and South America
- Tail can be more than twice the length of the body

Gray Four-eyed Opossum

- Lives in Central and South America
- Called four-eyed because of the white spots over its eyes

Patagonian Opossum

- Found only in Argentina, South America
- Females do not have a pouch

Opossum History

Opossums most likely came from early marsupials that lived in South America. Opossums first appeared in North America less than one million years ago.

In 1608, explorer John Smith came to North America. He used the word "opossum" to describe the animal. It comes from the American Indian word *apasum*, which means "white animal."

In letters to England, Smith wrote that the opossum had a head like a pig, the tail of a rat, and was about the size of a cat.

Fascinating Facts

Early relatives of the opossum lived during the age of the dinosaurs.

Opossums climb trees to escape predators. Opossums may hiss or screech if they feel threatened. They can also spray a smelly liquid.

Opossum Shelter

Opossums live in forests near streams. They can be found high up in trees or in hollow logs along the ground. Some live in abandoned, or empty, groundhog holes. Opossums' homes are called dens. They make nests of leaves in their dens.

A male opossum may roam an area of about 0.4 square mile (1 square kilometer) in size. This area is called his range. A female's range is only half that size. Within this range, an opossum may have many nests.

In cold winter weather, opossums do not **hibernate**. Instead, they stay in their den and do not move. After a few days, they will come out to search for food.

Opossums use their tail to carry nesting items, such as grass and leaves.

Opossums remain in their dens during the day. They are nocturnal, or most active at night. This is when they hunt for food.

Opossum Features

An opossum's body is suited to life outdoors. The opossum's feet and long tail are designed for climbing trees. Its numerous teeth allow it to eat and protect itself. Thick fur keeps opossums warm in winter.

TEETH

Opossums have 50 teeth in their mouth. They have more teeth than any other mammal in North America. The teeth help them chew. Opossums show their teeth to scare off enemies.

HAIR
An opossum's body is covered with long, thick fur. The underfur is soft and woolly. This fur helps keep the opossum warm.

FEET
The opossum has five toes, with claws on each of its front feet. Each hind foot has four clawed toes and an **opposable** thumb. This helps the opossum climb trees with ease.

TAIL
Opossums are very good climbers. They use their tail to ease up a tree branch.

What Do Opossums Eat?

Opossums are omnivores. This means that they eat both plants and animals. A main part of their diet is insects. They eat crickets, beetles, butterflies, worms, and grubs.

In spring, opossums feed on bird eggs or baby birds. Frogs, lizards, snakes, and small rabbits also are part of their diet.

Opossums eat a large variety of fruit and berries. If food is scarce, an opossum will travel out of its territory to find more.

Opossums eat grasshoppers.

Opossums have a keen sense of smell.
They use their sense of smell to search
for food, such as berries.

Opossum Life Cycle

Opossums begin to mate in mid-January and February. Mating continues into August. To attract a female, the male makes clicking sounds with his mouth.

Joey

An opossum baby is called a joey. A joey is about 0.5 inch (1.4 cm) long. This is the size of a honeybee. Joeys are not fully developed at birth. They must remain in their mother's pouch to survive. There, they feed on their mother's milk and begin to grow.

1 to 3 Months Old

After a few months, the babies will peek out of their mother's pouch. Some may ride on her back. By about three months, the baby opossum is **weaned**. It is ready to live on its own. If it is winter, the young opossums will travel with their mother.

Most female opossums can have up to two **litters** a year. There is usually about 110 days between litters. A litter may have as few as four or as many as 24 babies.

Adult

An opossum is full grown at one year of age. Most adult opossums weigh between 4 and 12 pounds (1.8 and 4.5 kilograms). Opossums usually live 2 to 4 years in nature.

Encountering Opossums

Sometimes, an opossum can become sick, injured, or **orphaned**. It may need human help. Still, opossums can bite if they feel threatened. It is important that an adult handle a hurt or orphaned opossum. You may need to call a veterinarian or wildlife officer for help.

An injured or orphaned opossum should be kept warm. This can be done by wrapping it in a blanket. The animal should be carefully placed in a box. A veterinarian will know what kind of care the opossum needs.

Useful Websites

To learn more about caring for an orphaned opossum, check out: **www.opossum.org/orphans.htm**

Sometimes opossums will climb trees onto rooftops. To stop this, keep trees well trimmed.

Myths and Legends

There are many stories about the opossum. One ancient myth explains why most opossums have hairless tails.

The opossum wondered how the raccoon got the rings on his tail. The raccoon explained that he wrapped bark around his tail. Then he dipped his tail into fire.

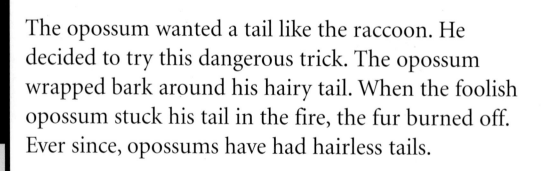

The opossum wanted a tail like the raccoon. He decided to try this dangerous trick. The opossum wrapped bark around his hairy tail. When the foolish opossum stuck his tail in the fire, the fur burned off. Ever since, opossums have had hairless tails.

The Opossum's Pouch

Here is a tale passed down by Louisiana's Koasati Indians.

One night, Mother Opossum was playing with her babies. Suddenly, Bat swooped down and carried the babies away. Mother begged for Bat to give back the babies. Bat ignored her. He put the babies in a deep hole and watched over them.

Mother Opossum cried for her babies. Wolf heard her cries and said he would help her. He walked into the forest, but he returned quickly. Wolf told Mother Opossum that he could not help her babies. She cried again. This time, Rabbit said he would get them for her. Rabbit walked into the forest, but he returned quickly. He told Mother Opossum that he could not get her babies. Mother Opossum was so sad.

An animal called Highland-Terrapin heard her cries. He went into the forest. Bat threw hot ashes at Highland-Terrapin's feet, but he kept going. Highland-Terrapin picked the babies out of the hole and returned them to their mother. To stop this from happening again, he made a hole in the belly of Mother Opossum and put the babies safely inside.

Frequently Asked Questions

Are opossums friendly?

Answer: Opossums are wild animals. They most often will shy away from people. If approached or handled, they may bite.

Is an opossum playing when it plays dead?

Answer: The opossum is not playing. It is frightened. Opossums pretend to be dead. They hope the predator will lose interest and walk away.

What does an opossum sound like?

Answer: An opossum makes a low, rumbling sound. It sounds like a running car motor. Mothers and babies make clicking sounds to locate each other. Males click to attract females during mating season.

Puzzler

See if you can answer these questions about opossums.

1. What is the most common opossum called?
2. How big is a baby opossum?
3. What is a marsupial?
4. What does an opossum do if it is cornered?
5. What do opossums eat?

Answers: 1. the Virginia opossum 2. the size of a honeybee 3. a type of mammal whose female most often has a front pouch on its stomach 4. plays dead 5. carrion, bugs, fruit, nuts, and bird eggs

Find Out More

There are many more interesting facts to learn about opossums. If you would like to learn more, take a look at these books.

Macken, JoAnn Early. *Opossums (Animals That Live in the Forest)*. Weekly Reader Early Learning Library, 2005.

Ripple, William John. *Opossums*. Coughlan Publishing, 2006.

Words to Know

habitats: the places where a plant or animal naturally lives

hibernate: to remain inactive for a long period of time

litters: babies born to one mother at the same time

mammal: a warm-blooded animal that has a backbone and drinks milk from its mother

opposable: able to move toward and touch other digits on the same hand or foot

orphaned: having no parents

predator: animals that hunt other animals for food

species: a group of animals or plants that have many features in common

weaned: stopped from drinking their mother's milk

Index